ELTON JOHN   THE DIVING BOARD

ISBN 978-1-4803-6443-1

HAL•LEONARD®
CORPORATION

7777 W. BLUEMOUND RD. P.O. BOX 13819 MILWAUKEE, WI 53213

Visit Hal Leonard Online at
www.halleonard.com

OCEANS AWAY

Words and Music by ELTON JOHN
and BERNIE TAUPIN

hung out with the old folks in the hope that I'd get wise. I was
bend like trees in win-ter, these shuf-fling old grey lions. Those

try-ing to bridge the gap be-tween the great di-vide. Hung on
snow-white stars still ga-ther like the great belt a-round Orion. Just to

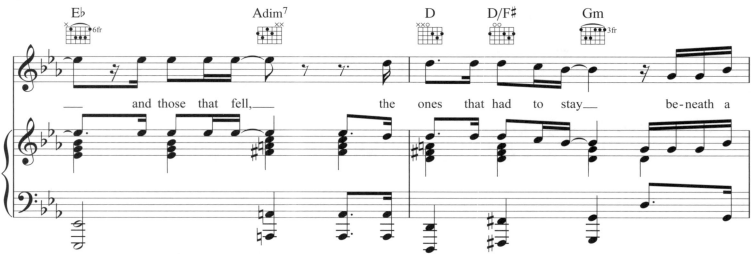

and those that fell,___ the ones that had to stay___ be-neath a

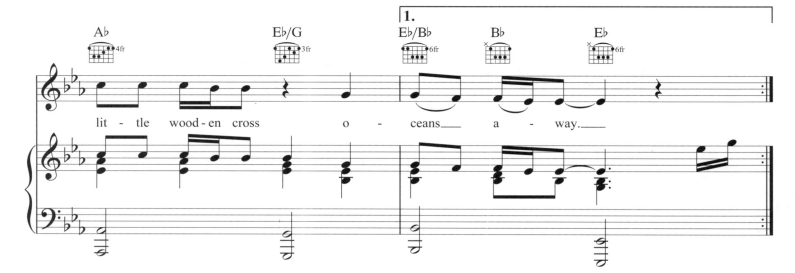

1.

lit - tle wood - en cross o - ceans___ a - way.___

2.

- ceans___ a - way.___

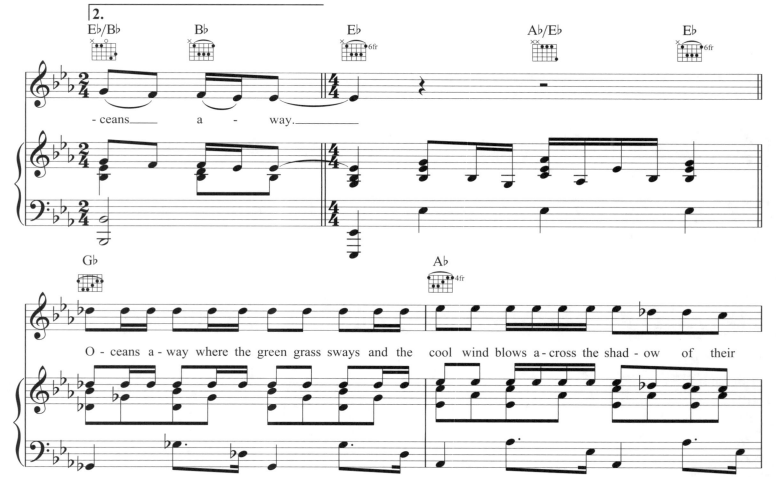

O - ceans a - way where the green grass sways and the cool wind blows a - cross the shad - ow of their

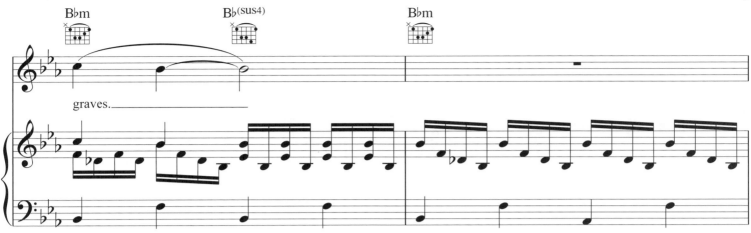

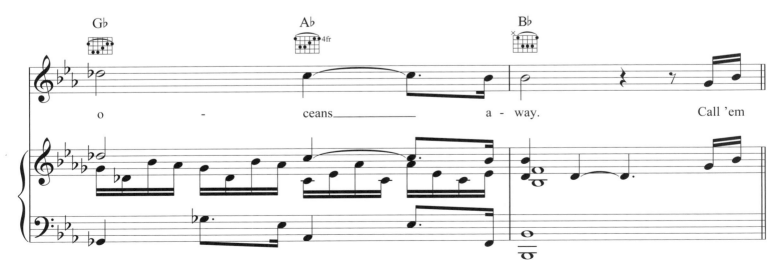

6

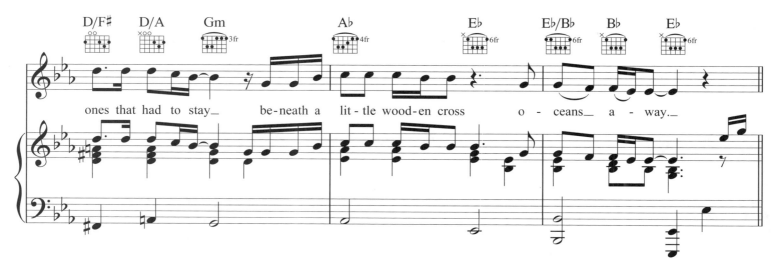

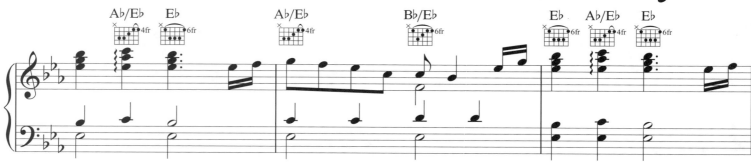

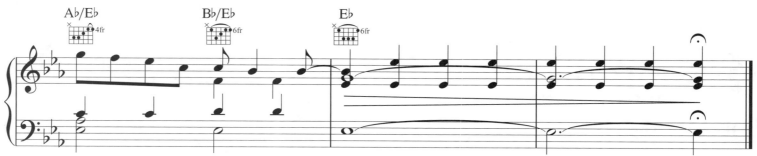

OSCAR WILDE GETS OUT

Words and Music by ELTON JOHN
and BERNIE TAUPIN

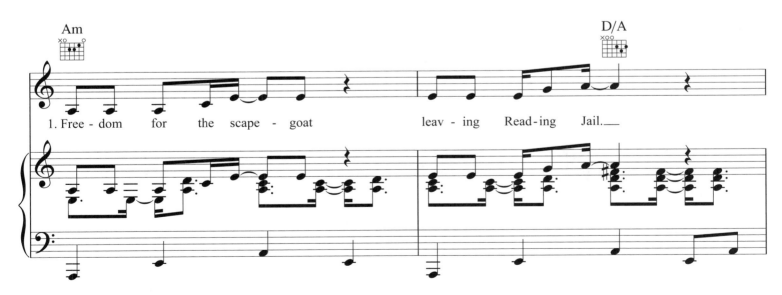

1. Free - dom for the scape - goat leav - ing Read - ing Jail.___

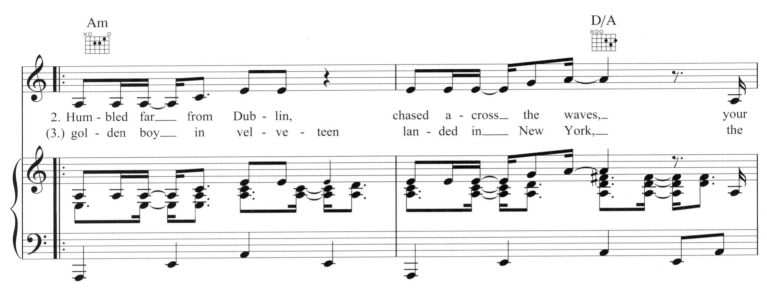

2. Hum - bled far___ from Dub - lin, chased a - cross__ the waves,___ your
(3.) gol - den boy__ in vel - ve - teen lan - ded in___ New York,___ the

bit - ing wit___ still sharp e - nough___ to slice through ev - 'ry page.___
past was so___ se - duc - tive_____ when they paid to hear you talk.___

Des - ti - tute___ and beat - en by___ the sy - stem of___ the crown,___ the
Bac - ca - rat___ and cham - pagne flutes,___ to - bac - co from___ Vir - gi - nia,

10

know - ing how___ love fools us all._____
in the arms___ of Sa - lo - me._____

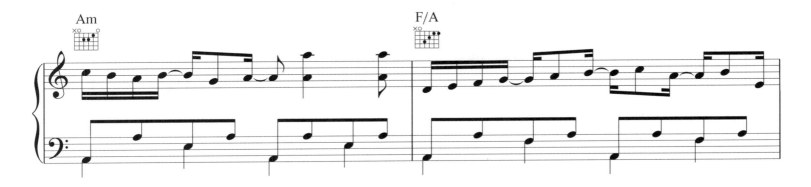

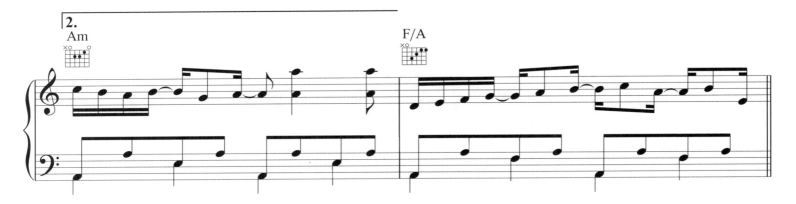

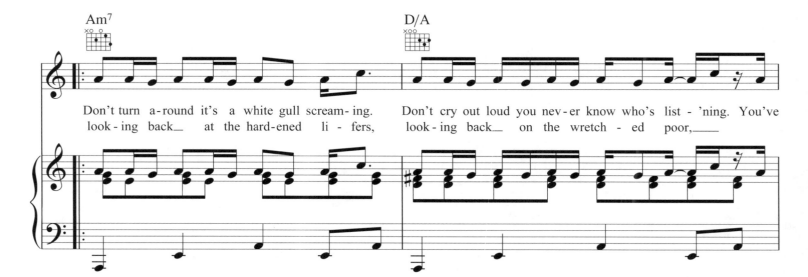

Don't turn a-round it's a white gull scream-ing. Don't cry out loud you nev-er know who's list - 'ning. You've
look-ing back__ at the hard-ened li - fers, look-ing back__ on the wretch - ed poor,__

seen it all__ the ex-iled Un-for-gi - ven.__ From the state -
think-ing may - be they__ were my sa - viors.__ Strange__

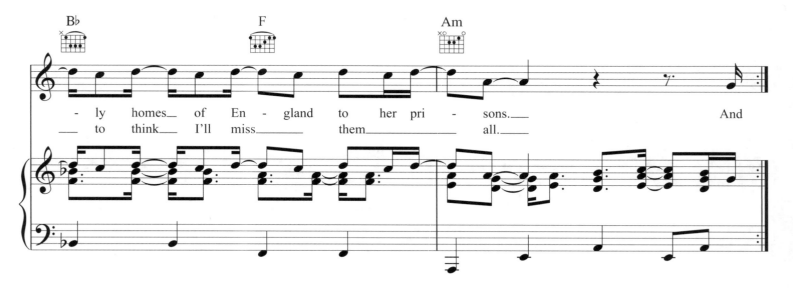

-ly homes__ of En - gland to her pri - sons.__ And
__ to think__ I'll miss_____ them_____ all.__

Strange to think__ I'll miss them all. And

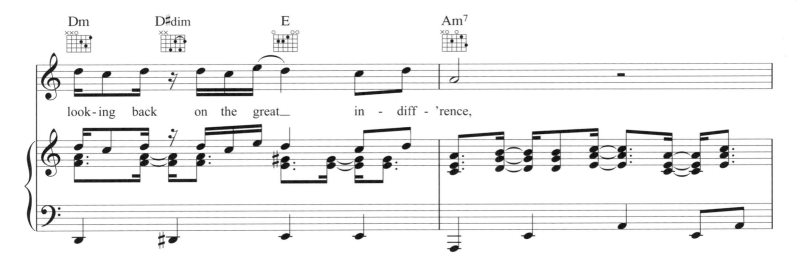

look-ing back on the great__ in - diff - 'rence,

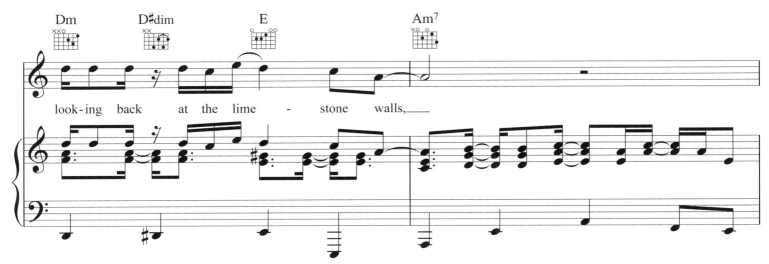

look-ing back at the lime - stone walls,__

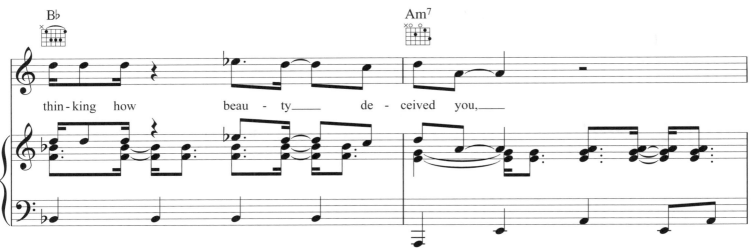

thin-king how beau - ty__ de - ceived you,__

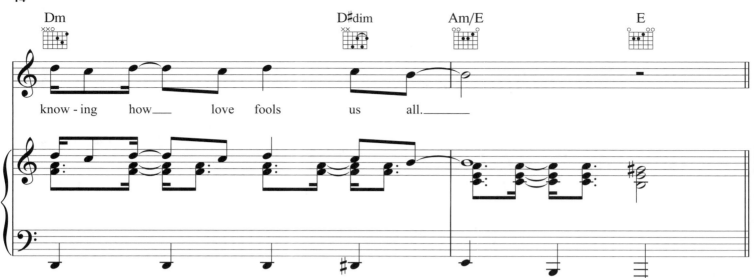

know-ing how___ love fools us all.___

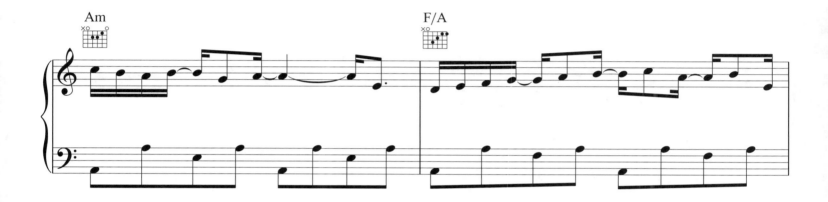

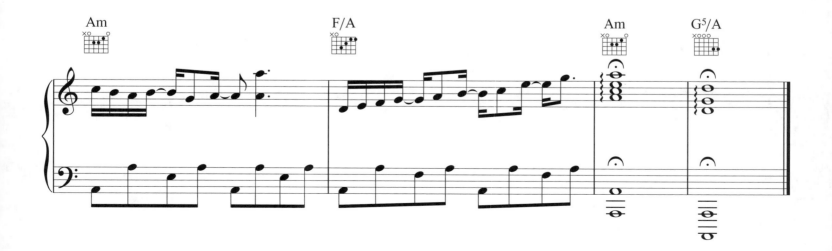

A TOWN CALLED JUBILEE

Words and Music by ELTON JOHN
and BERNIE TAUPIN

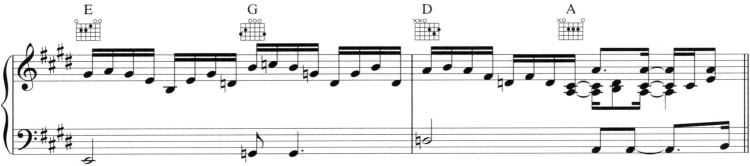

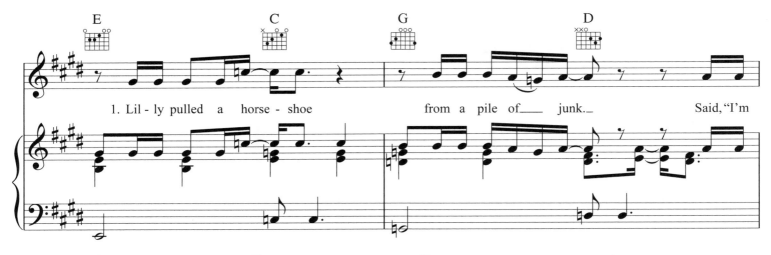

1. Lil-ly pulled a horse-shoe from a pile of___ junk.___ Said, "I'm

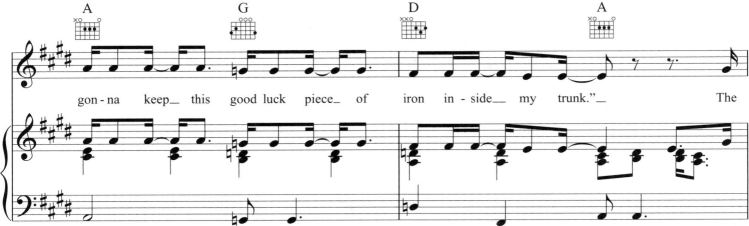

gon-na keep___ this good luck piece___ of iron in-side___ my trunk."___ The

boy just whis-pered "O___ K" and grabbed his old___ black dog,___ as we

piled on in___ and cut out through___ that late No-vem-ber fog.___

2. Dull as a plough - share rust-ing in the yard,___ old

3. That fire came out of no-where short of what I can tell. Hand to

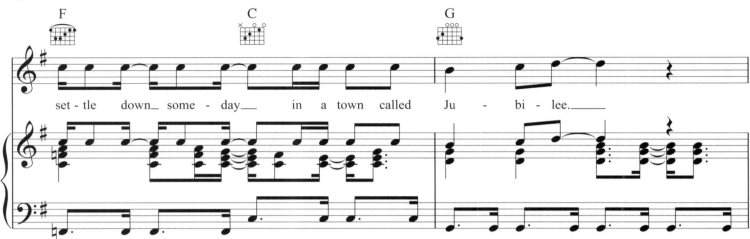

set - tle down__ some - day__ in a town called Ju - bi - lee.__

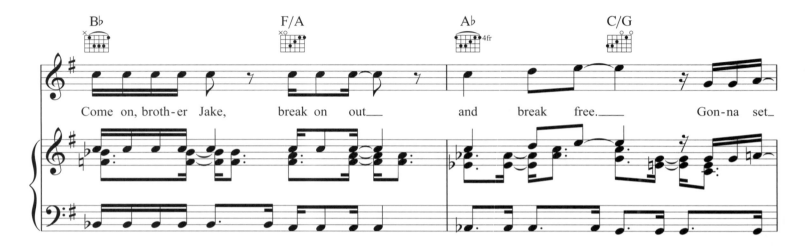

Come on, broth-er Jake, break on out__ and break free.__ Gon-na set__

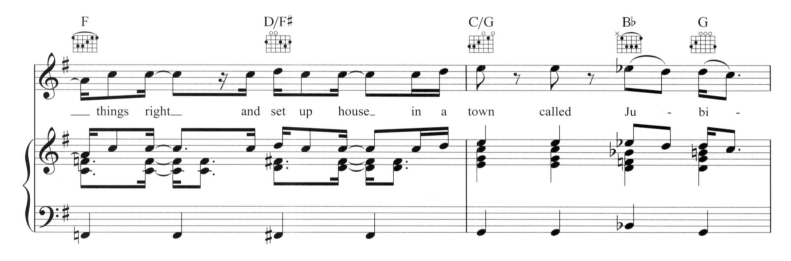

__ things right__ and set up house__ in a town called Ju - bi -

-lee. One last hal-le-lu-jah, a lit-tle less sym-pa-thy.__

Lil-ly and Jake,__ the old black dog,__ a pine-wood box, a rock-ing horse,__ all

gone to Ju - bi - lee.

Piano ad lib.

Come on, lit-tle sis-ter, get__ up off - a my knee. Gon-na

20

THE BALLAD OF BLIND TOM

Words and Music by ELTON JOHN
and BERNIE TAUPIN

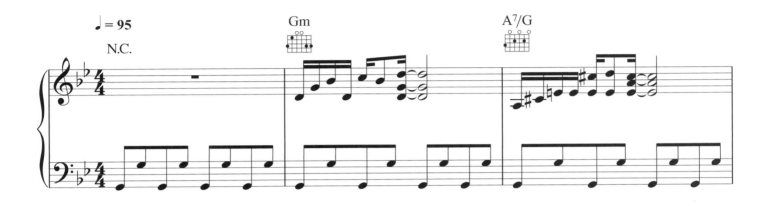

1. "Say

that boy's a won - der - ment."___ "No! The kid's a freak."___ But

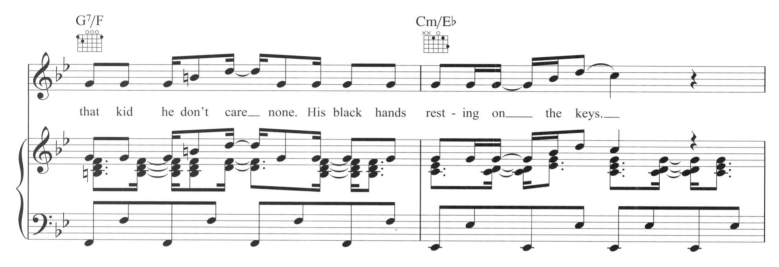

that kid he don't care___ none. His black hands rest - ing on___ the keys.___

Hop - pin' like___ a big old frog___ and his - sin' like a train.___

En - ter - tain - ing roy'l - ty, all points east, west and in - be - tween.___

2. Gen - 'ral, he's a fine old man,___
(3.) ___ that old big head a - side,___

treat him like his own.___ "Boy would - n't know from mon - ey" Just throw
grunts a word or two.___ Keeps 'em gues - sin' ev -'ry night: Is he

old Blind Tom a bone.___ From the times_____ of King Cot - ton may
real - ly gon - na make it through.___ Faint___ hearts with their fans out, starched

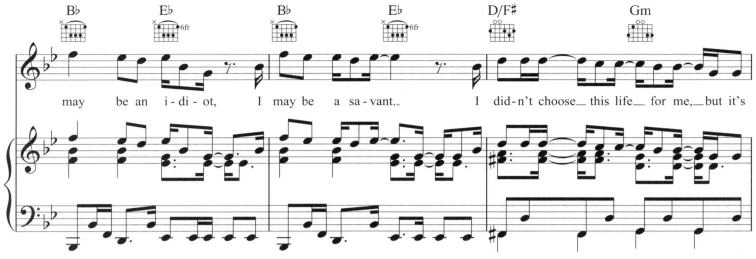

may be an i-di-ot, I may be a sa-vant.__ I did-n't choose__ this life__ for me,__ but it's

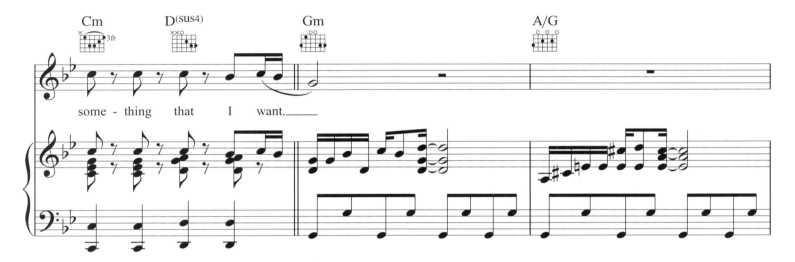

some - thing that I want._____

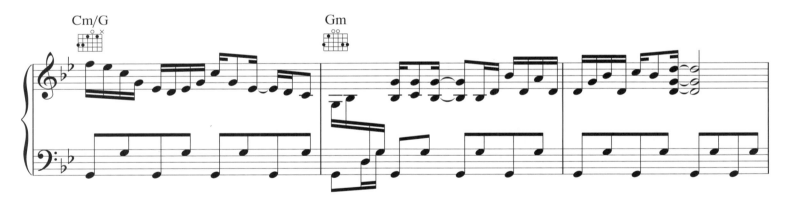

1.

3. Cocks__

Play me an - y - thing_ you like, I'll

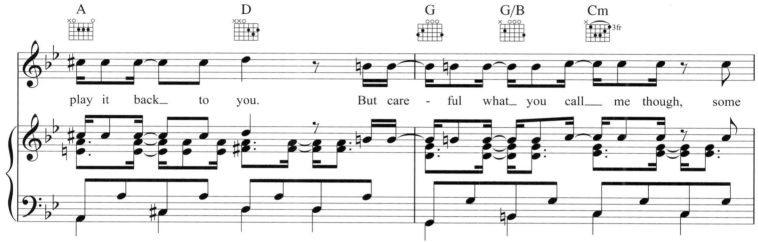

play it back_ to you. But care - ful what_ you call_ me though, some

things cut clear on through.___ I may be an i - di - ot, I

may be a sa - vant.___ I did - n't choose this life_ for me,_ but it's

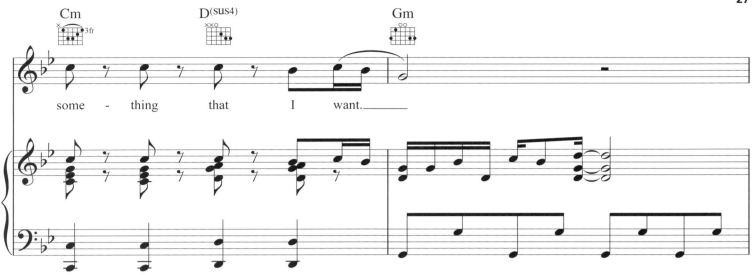

some - thing that I want._____

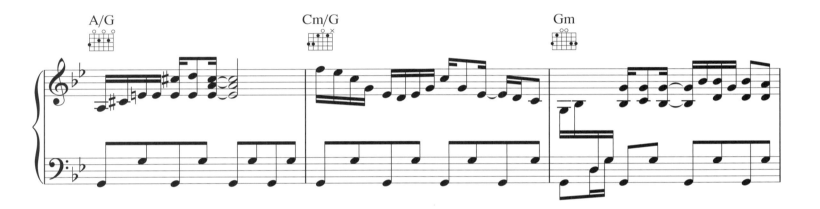

DREAM #1

Words and Music by ELTON JOHN
and BERNIE TAUPIN

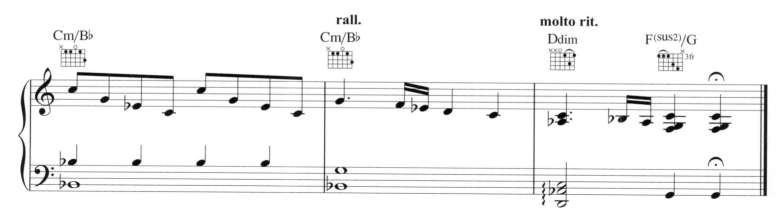

MY QUICKSAND

Words and Music by ELTON JOHN
and BERNIE TAUPIN

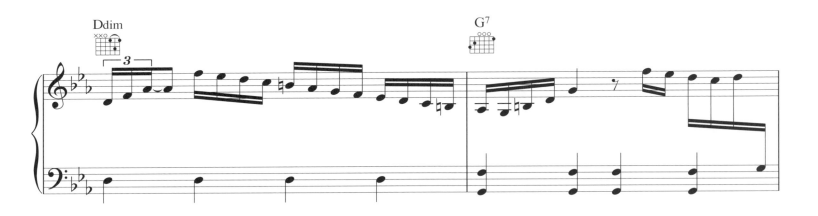

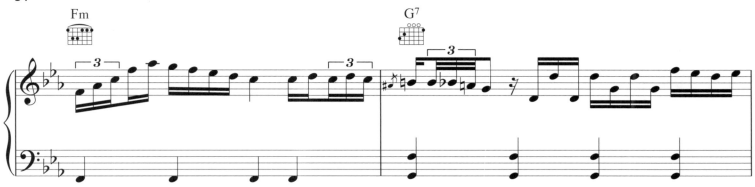

My quick -

sand,   let me in-tro-duce you to my fi-nal stand.   I went to

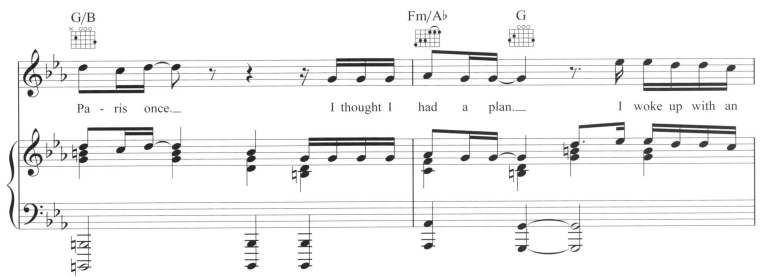

Pa - ris once.___ I thought I had a plan.___ I woke up with an

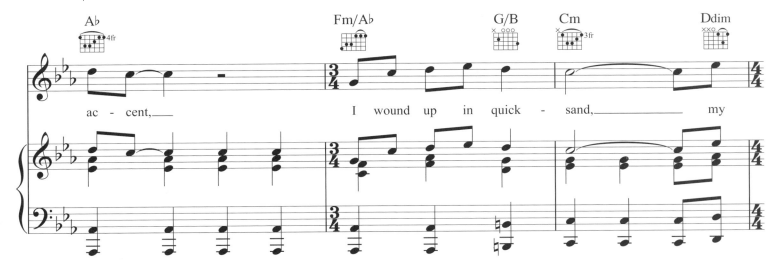

ac - cent,___ I wound up in quick - sand,_____ my

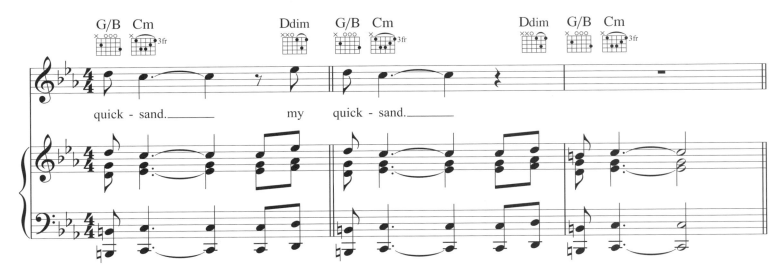

quick - sand.___ my quick - sand.___

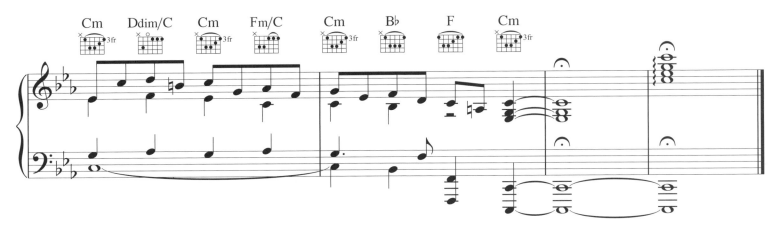

CAN'T STAY ALONE TONIGHT

Words and Music by ELTON JOHN
and BERNIE TAUPIN

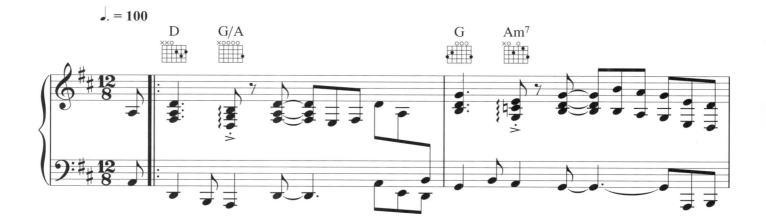

1. Blew the dust out of the cor - ners,_____
2. Chalk up one more cra - zy no - tion,_____

but I'm such a fool at times.
I'm that o - pen stretch of road.

I still search my shav - ing mir - ror,___
You're the di - ner in my rear - view,___

look - ing for your face with mine.___
a cup of cof - fee get - ting cold.___

And I

can't stay a - lone to - night. Can't let an - oth - er day go

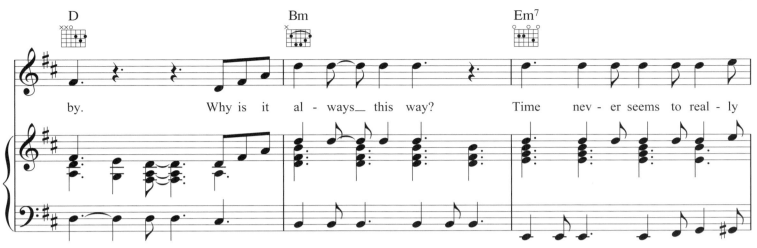

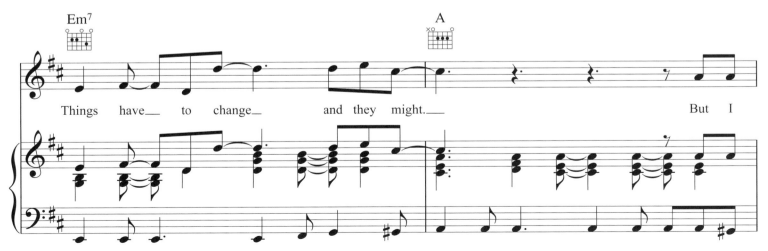

Things have___ to change___ and they might.___

But I can't stay a-lone to - night.___

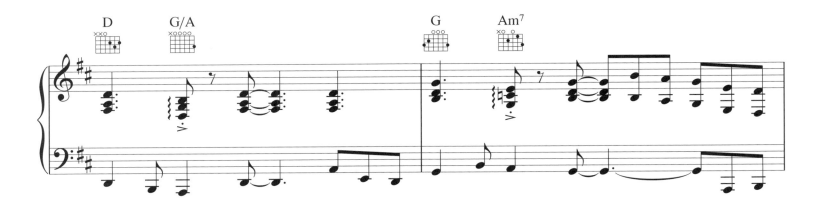

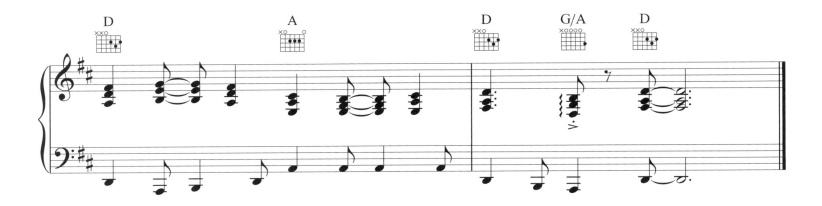

VOYEUR

Words and Music by ELTON JOHN
and BERNIE TAUPIN

look-ing,___ I'm look-ing back,___ I'm try'n' to i-ma-gine___ this and that. The
search-ing,___ I'm set-ting out___ to prove with-out a shad-ow___ of a doubt. The

- mit - ted to con-nect-ing the old____ ways to the new.____ And I see____ things through a
- lief that's tem-po - ra - ry from her dirt - y lit - tle war.____ And I see____ things from the

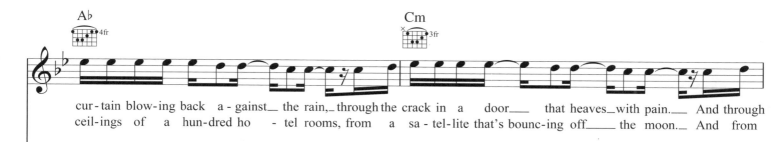

cur - tain blow-ing back a - gainst____ the rain,__through the crack in a door____ that heaves__with pain.____ And through
ceil-ings of a hun-dred ho - tel rooms, from a sa - tel-lite that's bounc-ing off____ the moon.__ And from

ev - 'ry gap__ that gives__ a - way__ some se - cret in__ the dark__)
ev - 'ry te - le - scope__ that's fo - cused in on some - place dark__)   I'll come a - way with

-li - cit lov - ers park__ I'll come a - way with some - thing__ to keep you in___ my

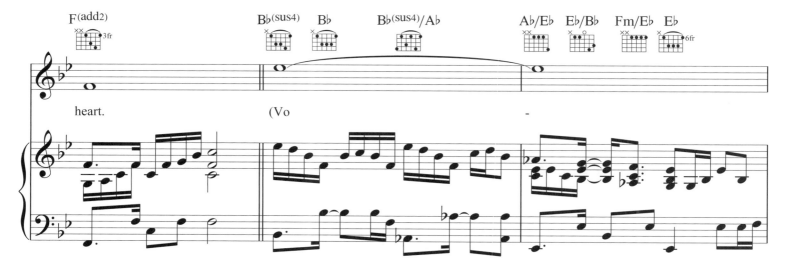

heart. (Vo -

- yeur.)_____

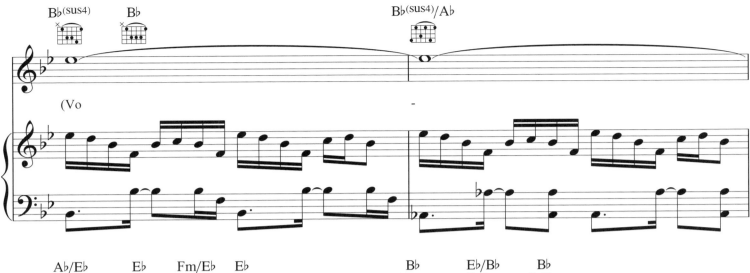

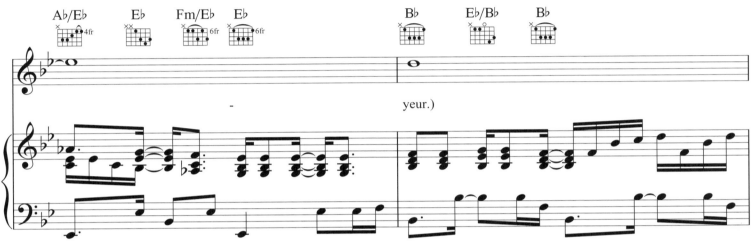

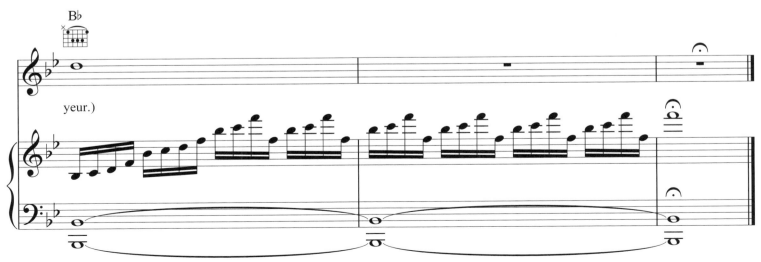

HOME AGAIN

Words and Music by ELTON JOHN
and BERNIE TAUPIN

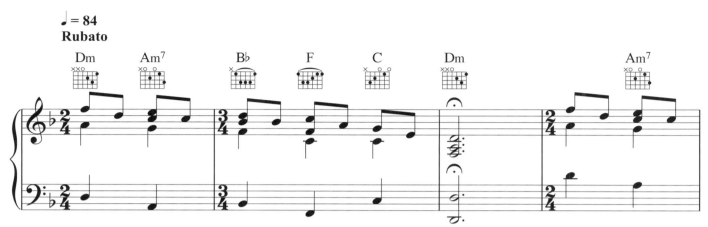

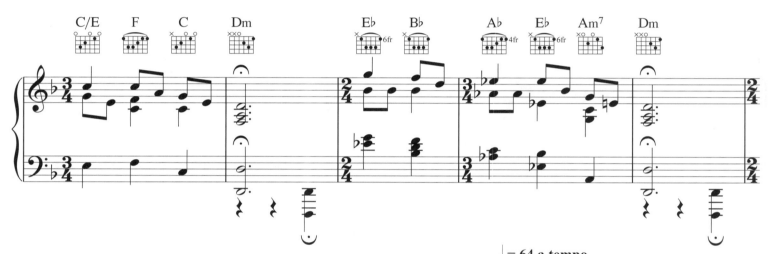

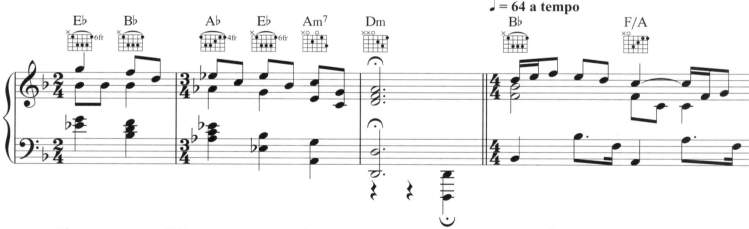

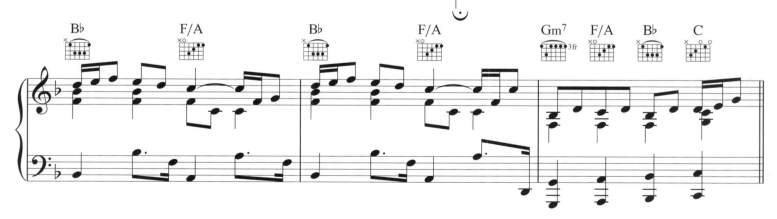

2. The world had sev-en won-ders once up-on a time.
3. Could have been a jail-break and the spot-light hit-ting me.

It's sure e-nough the fav-oured na-tions aid-ed their de-cline. And all a-
Or was I just some night-club sing-er back in nine-teen six-ty three? In the

round me I've seen times like it was back when. But like back
old part of Va-len-cia on the coast of Spain. Nev-er

then I'd say a-men if I could get back home a-gain. If I could
tir-ing once of hear-ing songs a-bout go-ing home a-gain.

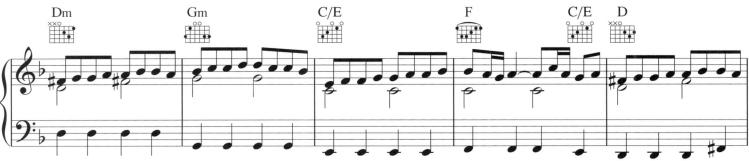

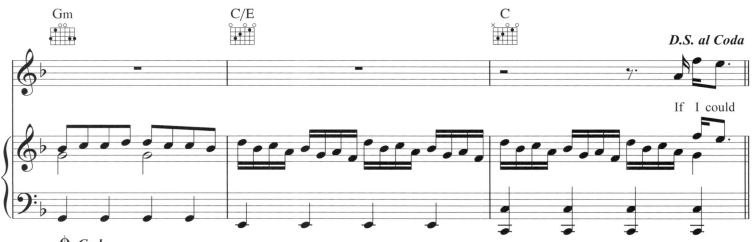

D.S. al Coda

If I could

Coda

- gain.

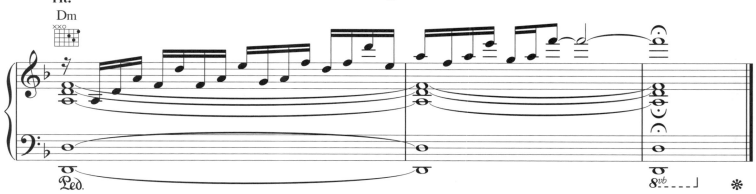

rit.

TAKE THIS DIRTY WATER

Words and Music by ELTON JOHN
and BERNIE TAUPIN

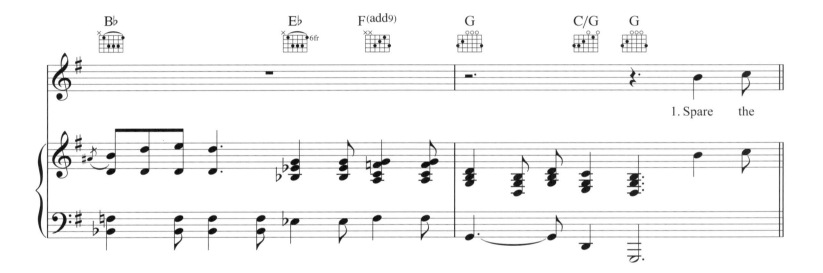

1. Spare the

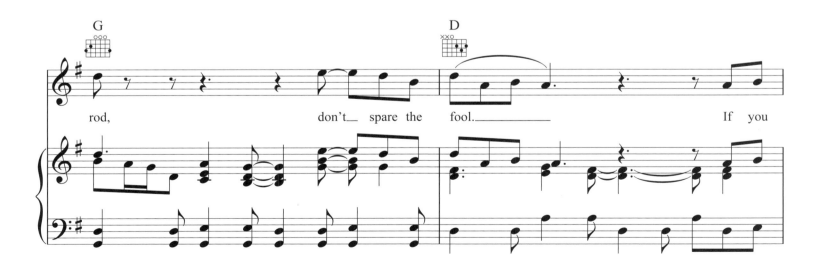

rod, don't___ spare the fool._____ If you

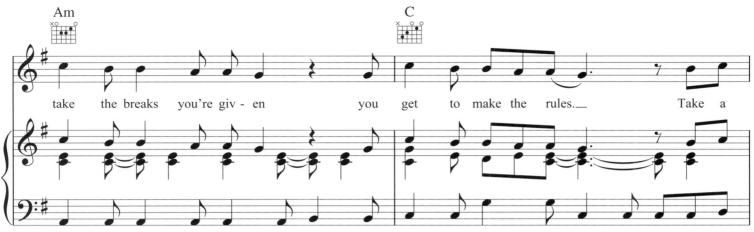

take the breaks you're giv - en you get to make the rules.__ Take a

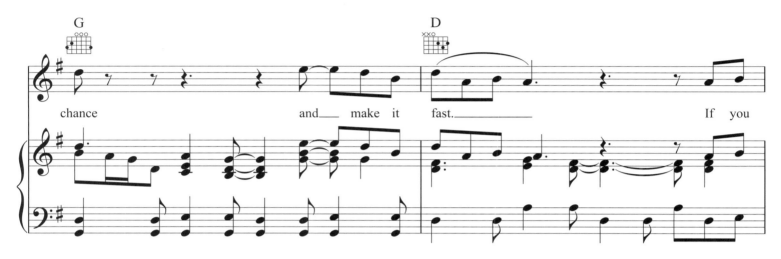

chance and__ make it fast._____ If you

break some bones on land - ing you know you're built to last.__ 2. Fight the

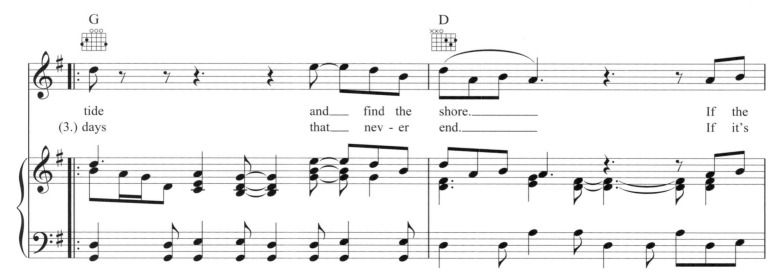

tide and__ find the shore._____ If the
(3.) days that__ nev - er end._____ If it's

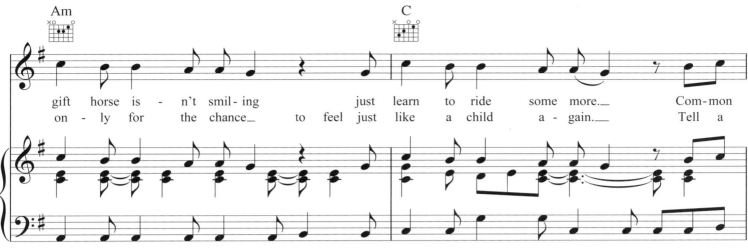

gift horse is - n't smil - ing   just learn to ride some more.___ Com - mon
on - ly for the chance___ to feel just like a child a - gain.___ Tell a

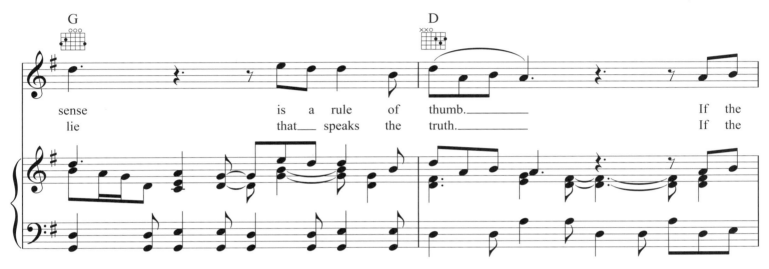

sense   is a rule of thumb._____ If the
lie   that___ speaks the truth._____ If the

suck - ers throw a red flag____   blow 'em all to King - dom Come._ } And
heart be - comes a pri - so - ner   your soul will turn you loose._ }

take   this dirt - y wa - ter_____   run - ning like a

riv - er_____ in_____ and out of

ev -'ry - thing we helped___ to put to - geth-er._____

Take_____ this dirt - y wat - er,_____

help___ to keep it clean.___ Get back to the well - spring,

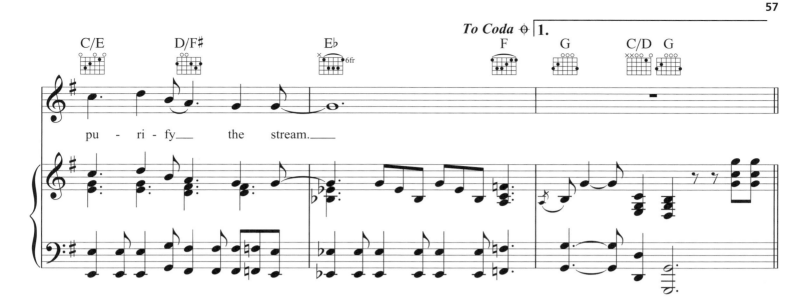

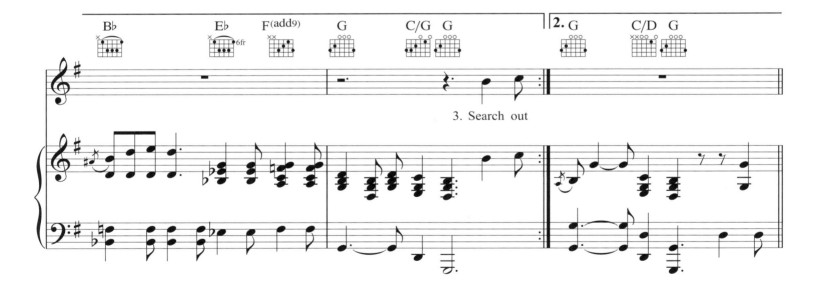

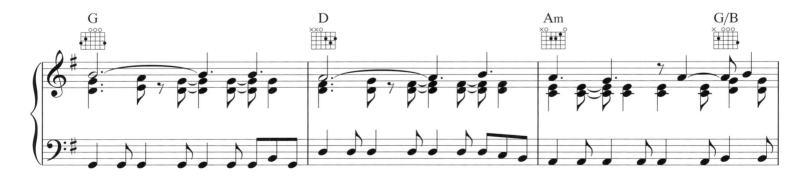

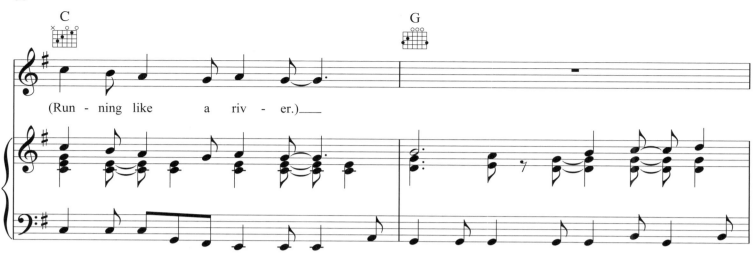

(Run - ning like a riv - er.)

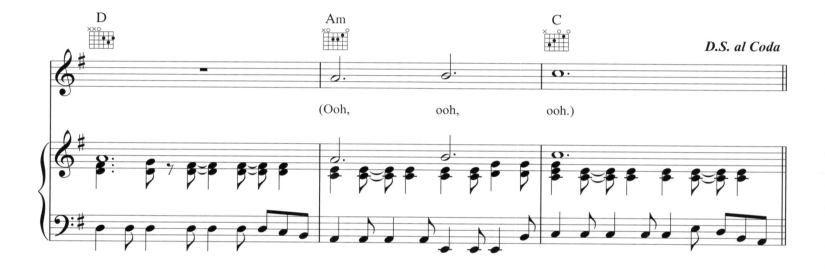

D.S. al Coda

(Ooh, ooh, ooh.)

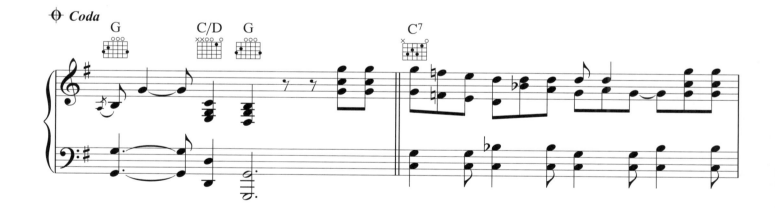

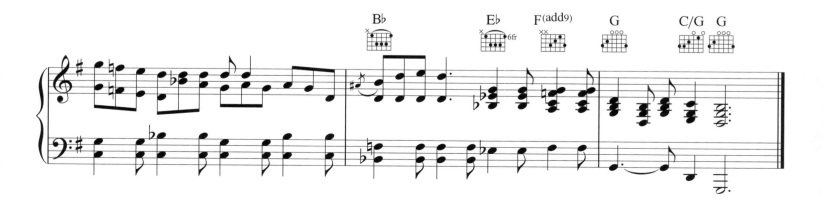

DREAM #2

Words and Music by ELTON JOHN
and BERNIE TAUPIN

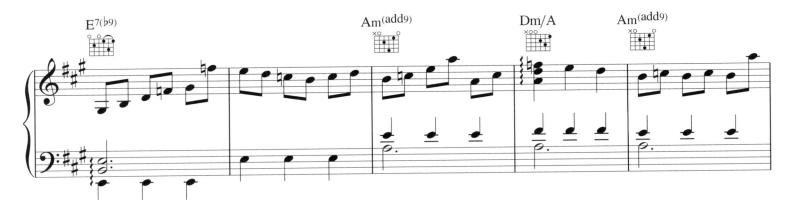

THE NEW FEVER WALTZ

Words and Music by ELTON JOHN
and BERNIE TAUPIN

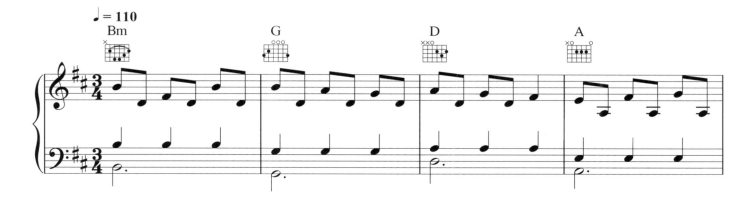

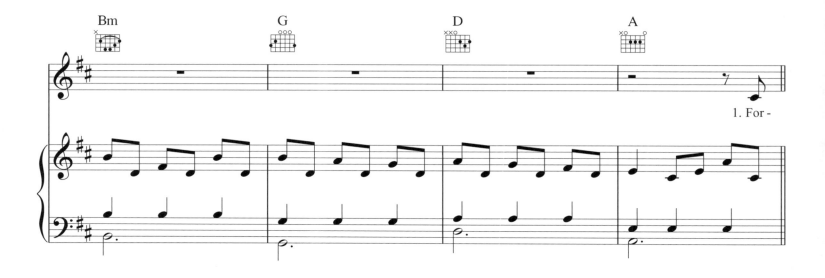

1. For -

-got-ten scars re-mind us of too much war, too lit-tle love. Be-neath the fault-line
2. Love in ru - ins, torn a-part, vic-tims of the care-less heart. Skat-ing on the

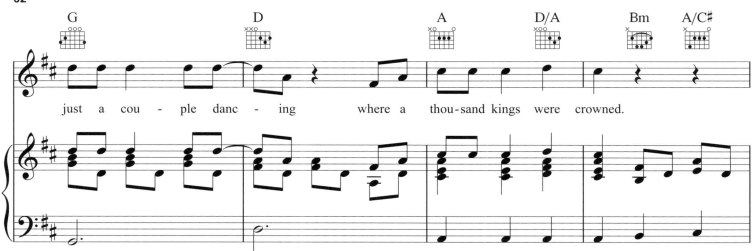

just a cou - ple danc - ing where a thou-sand kings were crowned.

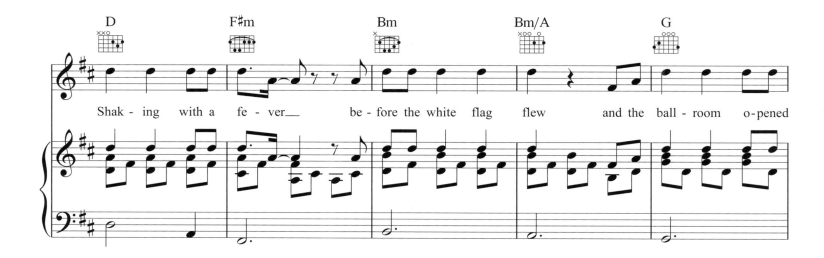

Shak - ing with a fe - ver___ be - fore the white flag flew and the ball - room o-pened

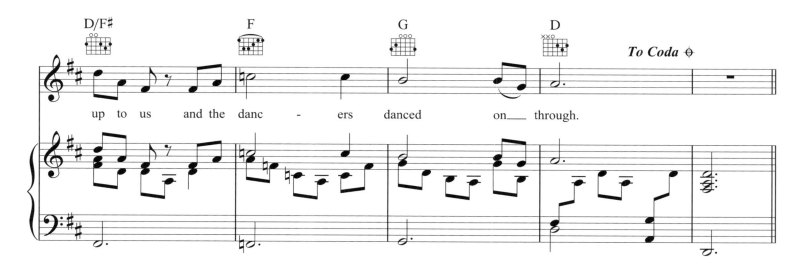

up to us and the danc - ers danced on___ through.

To Coda ⊕

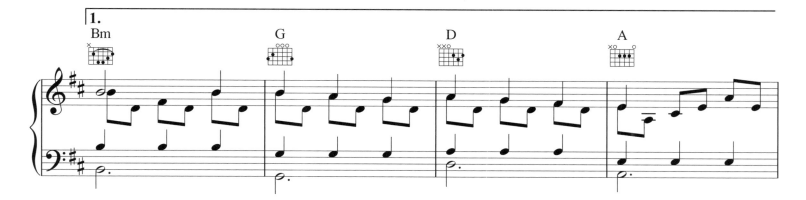

1.

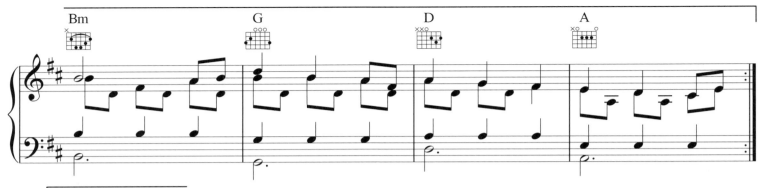

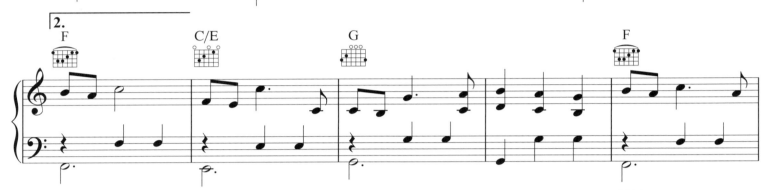

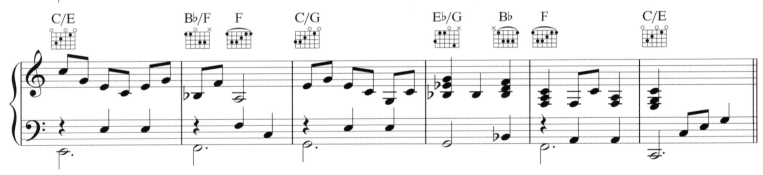

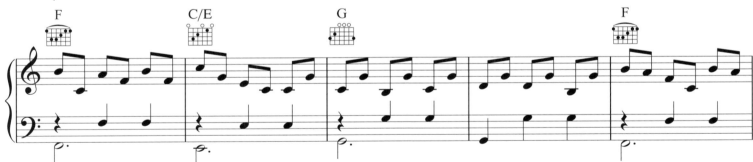

D.S. al Coda

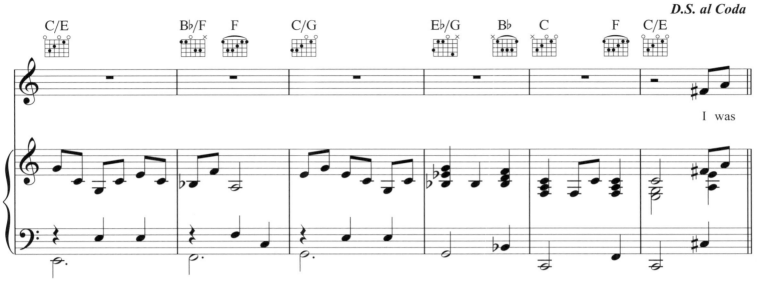

I was

Coda

And the danc - ers danced on___ through.

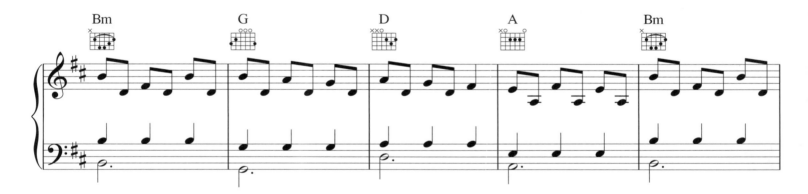

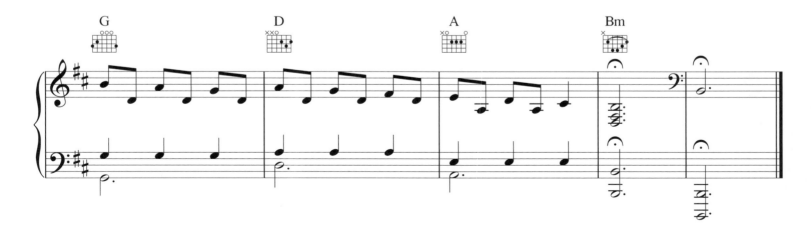

MEXICAN VACATION
(Kids in the Candlelight)

Words and Music by ELTON JOHN
and BERNIE TAUPIN

1. Oh,_____ I
2. Mm,_____ five

car - ried you in my arms___ through the ho - tel to our room.___ The
hun - dred wood - en saints be - low, their col - ours cracked and dry.___ You
(3.) pil - low that you dream on lies rolled up on the floor.___ You

66

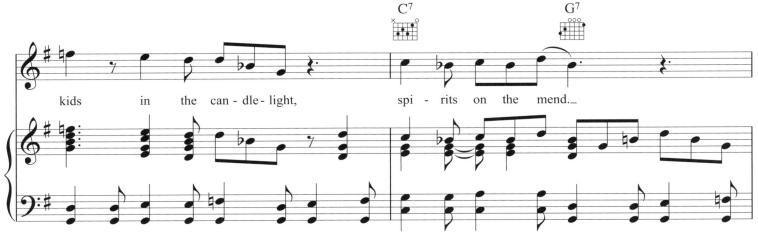

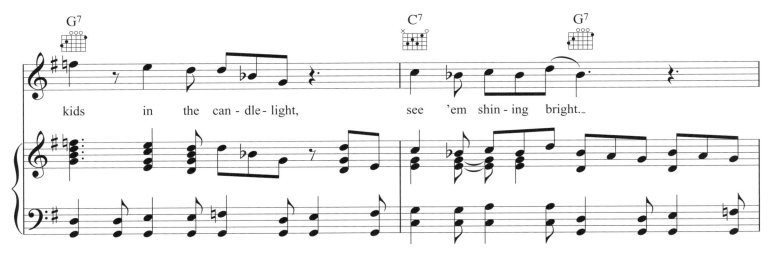

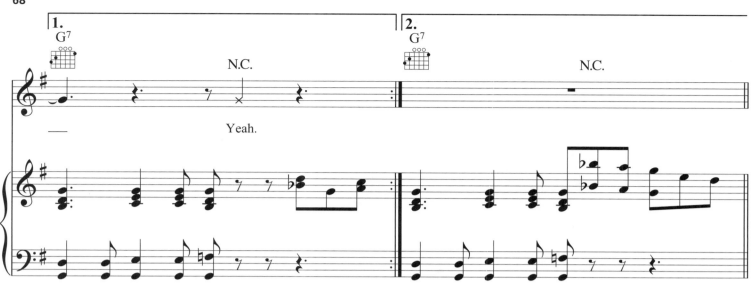

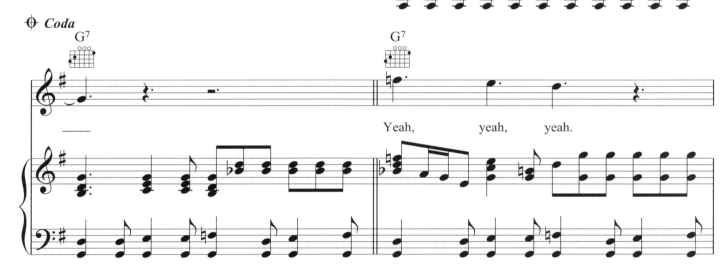

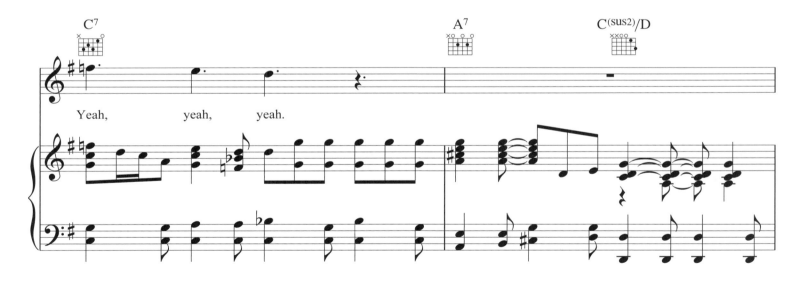

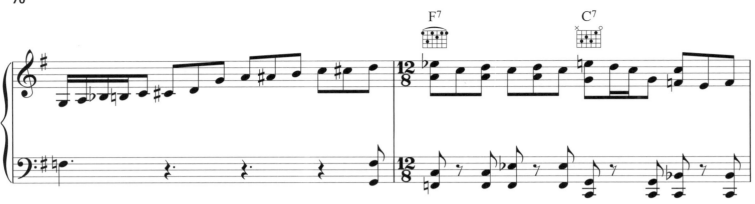

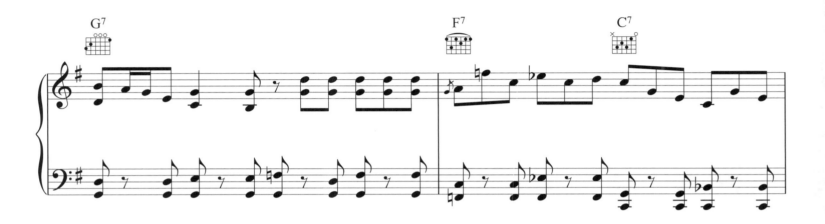

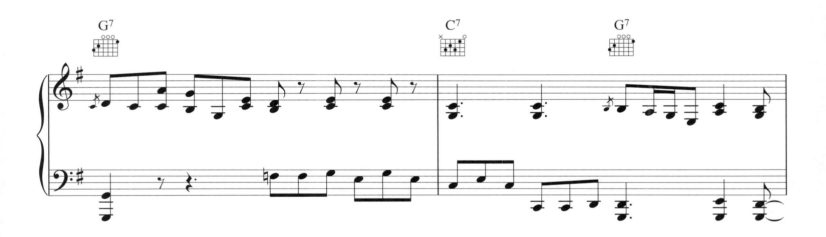

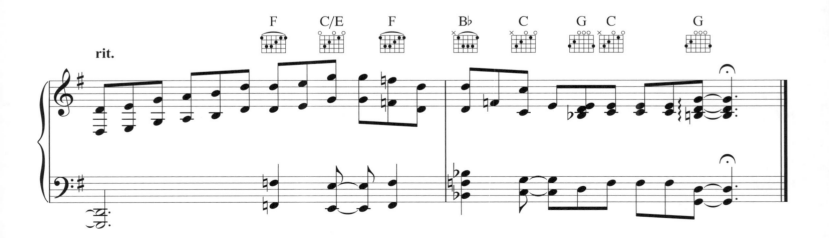

DREAM #3

Words and Music by ELTON JOHN
and BERNIE TAUPIN

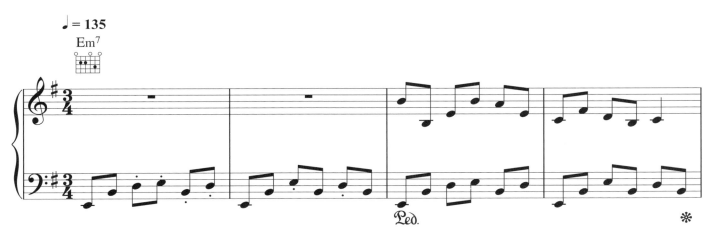

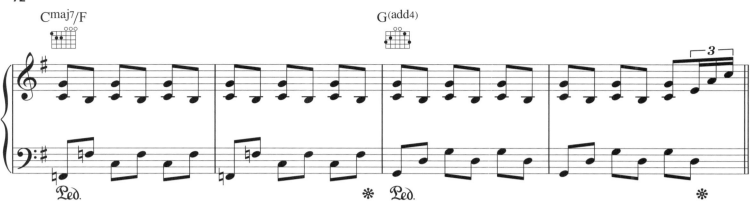

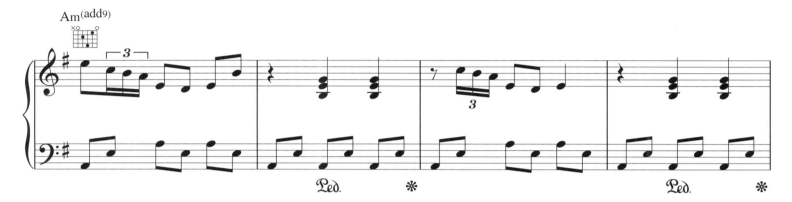

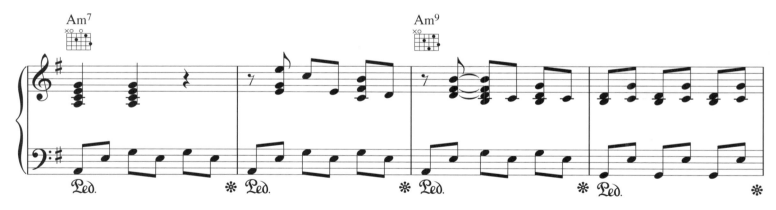

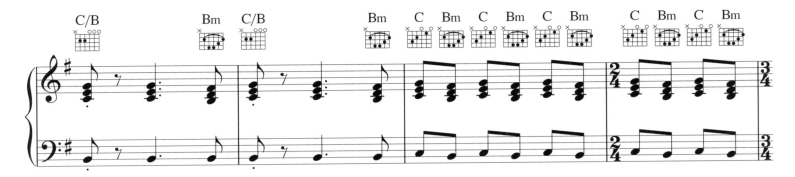

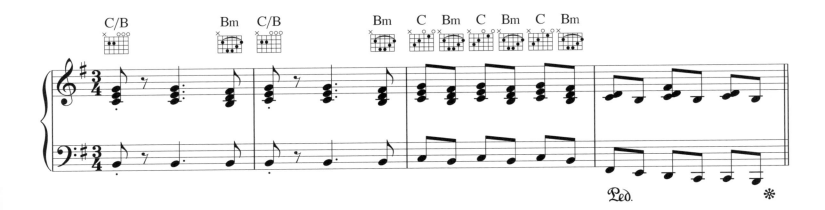

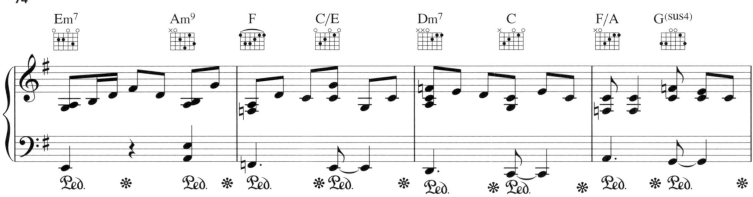

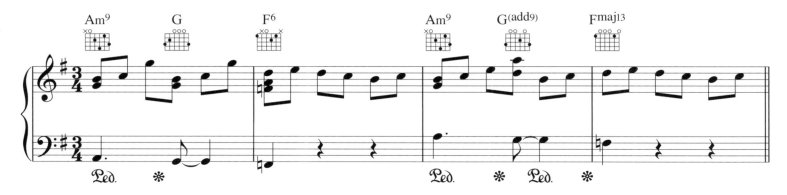

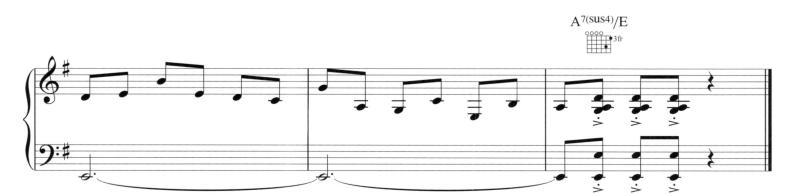

THE DIVING BOARD

Words and Music by ELTON JOHN
and BERNIE TAUPIN

from up there on the div - ing board.__
way up on the div - ing board.__
skin, high up on the div - ing board.__

1. **2, 3.**

2. You'd

Sink or swim__

I__ can't re - call__ who said that__ to me?__

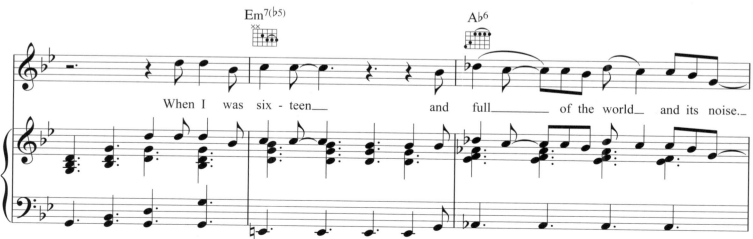

When I was six - teen__ and full__ of the world__ and its noise.__

But you_____ beat the drum._____ You fell in love___ with it

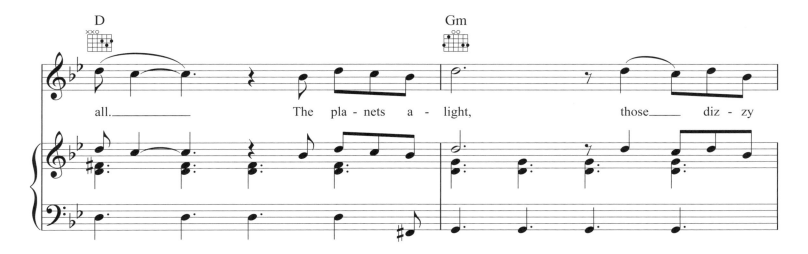

all._____ The pla - nets a - light, those_____ diz - zy

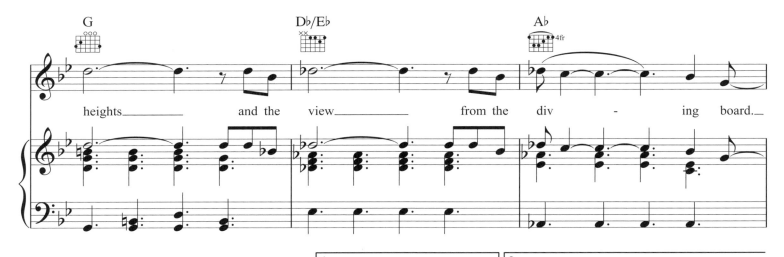

heights_____ and the view_____ from the div - ing board.___

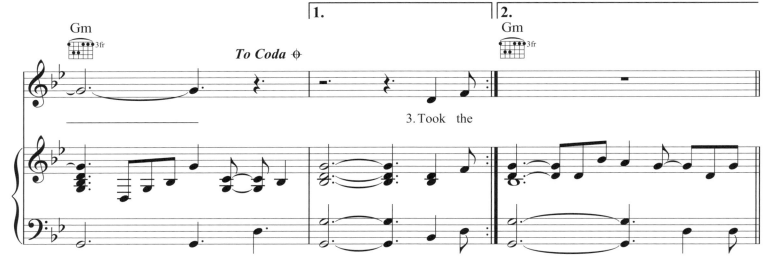

To Coda

3. Took the

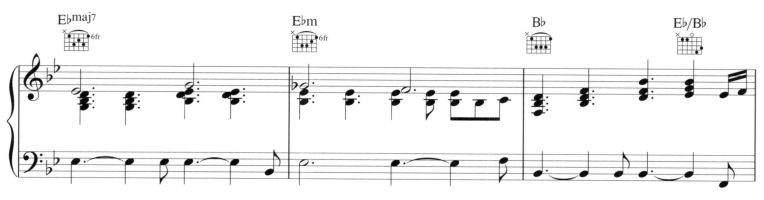

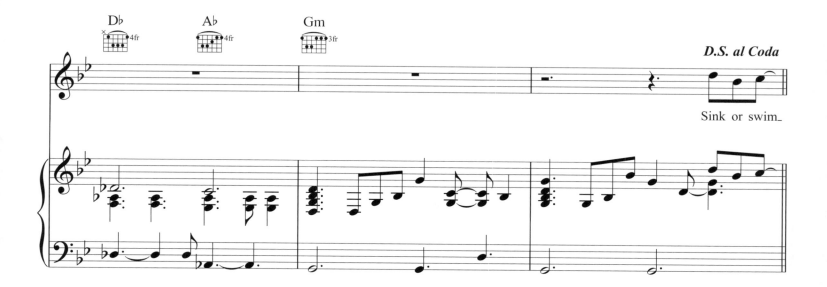

Sink or swim

And the view_____ from the

div - ing board._____

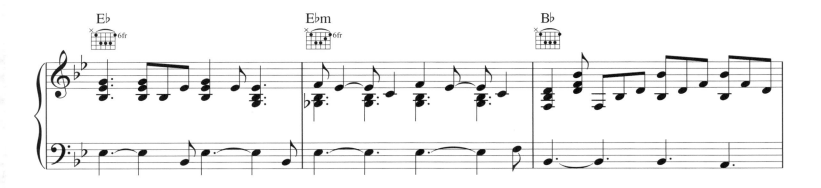

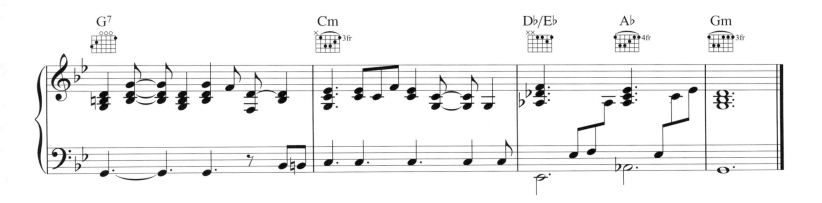